Janet Langhart Cohen's

ANNE & EMMETT

A One-Act Play
School Edition

Janet Langhart Cohen's

ANNE & EMMETT

A One-Act Play by
Janet Langhart Cohen

THEATRE & CINEMA BOOKS
Guilford, Connecticut

Applause Theatre & Cinema Books
An imprint of The Rowman & Littlefield Publishing Group, Inc.
4501 Forbes Blvd., Ste. 200
Lanham, MD 20706
www.rowman.com

Distributed by NATIONAL BOOK NETWORK

Copyright © 2006, 2013 by Langhart Communications, LLC
Copyright © 2021 by Anne & Emmett, LLC

This work, including the musical score, is fully protected by copyright. No alterations, deletions, or substitutions may be made in the work without the prior written consent of the author. No part of this work may be reproduced or transmitted in any form by any means—electronic or mechanical, including photocopy, recording, videotape, film, and digital means or via any information-storage and—retrieval system—without permission in writing from the author. The work, including the musical score, may not be performed either by professionals or amateurs without payment of royalty. All rights—including, but not limited to, the professional, motion picture, radio, television, videotape, foreign language, tabloid, recitation, lecturing, publication, and reading rights—are reserved.

Screenplay WGA #1303932 Play WGA 1303936

Library of Congress Control Number: 2020919399

Library of Congress Cataloging-in-Publication Data Available

ISBN 978-1-4930-5604-0 (paperback)
ISBN 978-1-4930-5900-3 (e-book)

*Dedicated to
Mamie Till-Mobley, Otto Frank, and all the parents
who have lost their children to violence and hate*

Racism is man's gravest threat to man—the maxim of hatred for the minimum of reason.

—Rabbi Abraham Joshua Heschel*

We will love them into their humanity, and we will shame them into their decency.

—Dr. Marin Luther King Jr.†

*For there is always light,
if only we're brave enough to see it,
if only we're brave enough to be it.*

—Amanda Gorman‡

---

*From Abraham Joshua Heschel's address made to the National Conference of Christians and Jews on Religion and Race, Edgewater Beach Hotel, Chicago, Illinois, January 14, 1963; subsequently published in Abraham Joshua Heschel, *The Insecurity of Freedom* (New York: Farrar, Strauss and Giroux, 1966), 85–100.
†From a conversation between Martin Luther King Jr. and and the author, 1966.
‡From Amanda Gorman's poem "The Hill We Climb" delivered at the inaugural of Joesph R. Biden as president of the United States, January 20, 2021.

CONTENTS

Janet Langhart Cohen's *Anne & Emmett*: A One-Act Play   1

Afterword: A Tree for Emmett Till   57

Score for *Anne & Emmett*: A Piece for String Orchestra and Piano, by Joshua Coyne (2009)   61

Acknowledgments   73

Student Guide   79

Janet Langhart Cohen's

ANNE & EMMETT

A One-Act Play

CAST
Anne Frank (Young Jewish girl, fifteen years old)
Emmett Till (Young Black boy, fourteen years old)
Otto Frank (Anne's father, mid-fifties businessman)
Mamie Till (Emmett's mother, mid-thirties educator)
J. W. Milam (One of Emmett's murderers, a white racist man, thirty-six years old)

(The theater is in complete darkness. The silence is broken by the sound of an oboe playing a sad melody, and then we hear a voice that is deep and sonorous, one that is from somewhere in the vast universe.)

VOICE-OVER: The struggle between good and evil has been with us a long time, and it's not likely to be going away any time soon. But I'd like to think that if we remember the past and some of the truly evil things we failed to stop, well . . . just maybe the good in us has a decent chance to survive.

Almost everybody knows the story of Anne Frank, the young Jewish girl who perished during Hitler's Holocaust. She left a diary that's inspired millions the world over. Fewer people know about Emmett Till, a young Black boy—just about the same age as Anne—who was tortured and lynched in Money, Mississippi, for whistling at a white woman. His brutal murder helped change the course of American history.

Imagine Anne and Emmett meeting in a place called Memory. What might they say to each other? Would they have anything in common to share? Or have any lessons for us? What happens if we don't listen to their voices? Are we doomed to simply repeat the past?

(A beat)

What if we don't even remember them?

(*Stage lights come up on* **MAMIE**, *a young Black woman who enters carrying a suitcase. She is young and has a pleasant face. She is dressed in a housedress and an apron that is cinched around her waist. While not overweight, she has a solid frame and roundness that convey a sense of a workingwoman's strength.* **MAMIE** *is packing the suitcase with shorts, shirts, and socks. There is a separate bag she's filling with sandwiches and water in a mayonnaise jar. She hums a Christian hymn, singing a few of its words . . .*)

MAMIE: . . . Swing low, sweet chariot . . .

Lord, good Lord. I don't know why I ever agreed to let him go down there to Mississippi . . . I got a bad feeling about this.

(**EMMETT**, *a young Black boy, dressed in a blue shirt and tan slacks held up by a pair of braces, races onto the stage, nearly out of breath. He's carrying a baseball glove and is pounding his fist into the glove.*)

EMMETT: Momma, you still packing? Everybody's ready to go . . .

MAMIE: Bo, come here for a minute . . .

EMMETT: Come on, Momma.

MAMIE: I said come here, Son. We need to talk.

EMMETT: Talk? Talk about what, Momma?

MAMIE: I want to be sure you understand what I said about how to behave down South.

EMMETT: Momma, you already told me.

MAMIE: Bo, listen to me. The rules are different for colored people down South. Don't go fooling around and acting all playful around white folks. They won't understand. They'll think you're being disrespectful, acting uppity . . . You need to understand—if you find yourself around white folks, stay quiet. If you see a white man coming down the street, look down. Don't look him in the eye.

EMMETT: Momma. You already told me this . . .

MAMIE: If he seems like he's going to walk past you, step off the sidewalk.

EMMETT: What if he speaks to me?

MAMIE: You just say, "Yes, sir."

EMMETT: Yassah! Yassah!

MAMIE: Now, Bo, this is serious. Don't you go playing around like that. You can do that in Chicago, but down there that can get you in real trouble, can—

EMMETT: I was just kidding, Momma. I won't do anything like that.

MAMIE: You're my baby, Bo. You're all I got in this whole world, but not everybody loves you like I do.

EMMETT: I'll be real polite. I promise.

MAMIE: Now, if you encounter a white woman, don't look at her. Don't say anything . . . If she comes to pass you on the sidewalk—

EMMETT: I know. Look down . . .

MAMIE: *No*, Bo. You don't just look down. You cross the street.

EMMETT: Okay, okay. I got it. Can I go now?

(A car horn blows offstage.)

MAMIE: Hold your horses. He'll be out in a minute . . . Bo, I want to be sure you understand the rules.

EMMETT: I know all the rules, Momma.

(A car horn blows again.)

Mamie: I said he'll be out in a minute! How many times you gonna blow that horn? . . . Bo, I love you more than I can say. Now, you promise your momma you'll do what I tell you?

Emmett: Yes, Momma; don't worry about me. I'll be a good boy.

Mamie: I know you're a good boy. It's just that—

Emmett: Don't worry, Momma. I won't be gone long. The summer will be over before you know it . . . I'll be with my cousins, and Uncle Mose will take good care of me . . . Gotta go now.

Mamie: Wait a minute, Bo. I got something for you.

Emmett: What?

Mamie: I was saving this for your twenty-first birthday, when you become a man. But I want you to have it now . . . Bring you some good luck.

Emmett: Wow! My father's ring. I can wear it? Can't wait to show it to everyone . . . Thank you, Momma. It's gonna be my lucky charm . . . You wait and see, Momma; one day I'm going to do something important, something big. I'm gonna make you real proud of me. You'll see—I'm going to be somebody.

Mamie: Bo, you're already somebody . . . Now give your momma a big hug. Take these sandwiches and water with you, because they won't be giving Negroes anything to eat on the train.

Emmett: Okay, Momma. I understand. Gotta go now.

> (*Mamie packs his baseball glove in the suitcase and snaps it shut; hands him the suitcase and box of food. She hugs Emmett again in a tight, longing embrace and kisses his forehead. Finally, she lets him go, and he dashes offstage. Seconds pass, and Emmett comes back onstage.*)

Momma, you seen my hat?

MAMIE: *(Holding the hat behind her back)* You mean this old thing?

EMMETT: You know it's my favorite. *(Reaching behind MAMIE's back, he playfully pulls on her apron string, causing her apron to fall loose.)*

MAMIE: Bo! You little devil . . . Okay, here it is. You'll need it to keep the sun off that pretty face of yours . . . Try to stay out of the sun.

(She places the hat on EMMETT's head and hugs him one last time.)

EMMETT: Okay. I love you, Momma. Bye.

MAMIE: I love you too, Bo. Remember now, be good . . .

(EMMETT exits stage. The car horn blows twice, signaling goodbye.)

I hope he'll be good. It's just that he's a boy and . . . well . . . Now I want him to see his uncle and his cousins, but why can't they come up here to visit? . . . I hope I didn't spoil it for him by telling him what he can't do or how to act. I don't want to break his spirit. But I couldn't just let him go without telling him the truth about the way they treat colored people. If anything were to happen to him, I'd never forgive myself . . .

(MAMIE walks upstage as it fades to darkness.

Stage right. The lights come up on ANNE, a young girl of about fifteen years of age who is dressed in a pretty wool skirt, dark sweater, and white frilly blouse. She is on a riser, stage right, sitting at a desk. On the desk is her plaid covered diary. She is deeply engaged in writing on a pad of paper. She surveys the page she has just written, decides she doesn't like it, and tosses it toward a trash receptacle. It misses and falls to the floor. She begins to write again.

OTTO, *a tall man, dressed in a white shirt, vest, and tweed-patterned pants, enters the room. He has an aristocratic bearing about him, and the dark-framed glasses that rest on his strong, prominent nose convey a sense that he is a learned man.* OTTO's *shoulders are slightly stooped, as if they carry the weight of the world. His face is lined with a crowd of sorrows, but he pretends that he is carefree.)*

OTTO: So how is my sweet little girl doing today?

ANNE: Fine, Poppa.

OTTO: Your writing is going well?

ANNE: Yes, Poppa.

OTTO: It's good that you have extra paper . . .

ANNE: I misspelled a word, and I want it to be perfect.

OTTO: Have you looked outside? It's getting dark. I think it might rain again today, but tomorrow the sun is going to—

ANNE: Poppa, since when do you want to talk with me about the weather? It doesn't matter if it's cloudy or sunny, if it rains or shines. It doesn't change anything in here . . .

OTTO: I was just trying to—

ANNE: Why don't you say what you're really thinking? Mother sent you up here, didn't she?

OTTO: Oh, Annelies. So you see through me again, hem? Sometimes I think you're too smart.

ANNE: Too smart? Isn't that what you've always wanted me to be?

OTTO: You know what I mean when I say "too" . . .

ANNE: So I should just remain smart?

Otto: I take it things did not go well today with your mother?

Anne: You know the answer, Poppa. It never goes well with Mother. She's always criticizing me. I never do anything that pleases her. She doesn't like me. Margot can do no wrong. Margot is her favorite . . . Poppa, am I your favorite? Tell me that I'm your favorite and you love me more . . . Please, Poppa.

Otto: I love you both Anne. Equally. Just as your mother does. She likes you, and she loves you. You misunderstand her. You're too hard on her.

Anne: She could be like you, Poppa. You understand me. I know you love me. Really love me. Just the way I am . . .

(The sound of someone pounding on a door below interrupts. The pounding grows more persistent. Otto and Anne freeze in place and hold their breath, as if the mere sound of their breathing could lead to their discovery. Then a police siren is heard in the distance. It grows louder as it approaches and then grows faint again. Both the pounding and the siren fade as Otto and Anne exhale, relieved that that the police and the people below were not coming for them.)

Anne: Poppa, how much longer do we have to live like this, trapped in this . . . this box? And with all of these other people!

Otto: These "other people" are our friends, Anne. They are at risk of being arrested, just as we are, and sent off to those horrible camps that we keep hearing about.

Anne: We're living in . . . a coffin. I can't stand it much longer, Poppa. I need to go out, be with my friends, ride my bicycle, be free, if only for an hour or two.

Otto: Anne, you know the rules. That's impossible. We can never go outside or be seen. Not until the Nazis are defeated. We can't—

Anne: Yes. The rules. Always the rules. No laughing, no joking, no talking, no fighting . . . no joy whatsoever. This is not living.

Otto: It is not living, but we are still alive! That's what you have to keep remembering, Anne. We are still alive.

Anne: But, Poppa, how much longer do we have to wait?

Otto: Not much longer. The British and the Americans will come. I'm sure of it. We continue to get reports. Soon they will come for us. We just have to be a little more patient.

Anne: I want to be a writer, Poppa, a famous one. Yes, I write all of my private thoughts in the diary you gave me, but I want so much more. I want to write novels, poems, plays. I can't do that all cramped up here. I need to be free.

Otto: I know, Anne. I know how talented you are. One day you'll be free, and you will touch the sky with your pen. People the world over will read you. But right now, it is too dangerous for any of us to be seen or heard.

(He wraps his arms around Anne in a warm embrace and gently strokes her hair.)

You're my precious little angel, and I will always protect you. I'll never let them harm you.

Anne: You promise?

Otto: I promise. And one day, you'll see, all of your dreams will come true. I promise.

(Otto walks to center stage as the lights fade on Anne.)

I don't know how much longer we can hide. The Gestapo are getting closer to us all the time. I know what they'll do if they find us . . . I served as an officer in the German army once . . . Lot of good that would do me . . . Get me a medal on my way to the gas chamber . . . If the Americans don't get here soon, then . . . But I can't speak the truth. Hope is the only thing that we have left . . .

> *(The stage lights fade to darkness. While the stage is still in darkness, a violinist begins to play an evocative musical theme. The stage lights come up and focus on ANNE. She is sitting at her desk, deeply engaged in writing on a notepad. She tears a sheet out and attempts to toss it into a trash receptacle. Once again, she misses, and the page falls to the floor.*
>
> *The violinist bridges to a variation on the musical theme. Seconds pass before additional lights illuminate EMMETT, who tumbles onto the stage, staggers to regain his balance, and starts to touch his face and body, as if to see if he is whole.*
>
> *The music stops.)*

ANNE: Who are you? How did you—

EMMETT: *(Angry and scared)* Me? No, you! You stay away from me . . . Go away!

ANNE: No! I live here. You're the one who has to go. You don't belong here. You— you . . . scared me!

EMMETT: Oh, I see. I scared you because I'm Black!

ANNE: Your color has nothing to do with it. I'm always here alone, by myself. You startled me the way you came breaking in here. For a moment, I thought you were the Dutch police coming for me.

EMMETT: Do I look like a Dutchman to you?

ANNE: Nooo. No, you don't. But why are you so hostile? I don't even know you.

EMMETT: You don't have to know me. That's the problem.

ANNE: What problem?

EMMETT: You're a white girl, and in Money, Mississippi, that means you can hurt me without saying a word. All you have to do is point a finger at me.

ANNE: Wait a minute. Who said anything about hurting you or Mississippi? We're here in Memory.

EMMETT: Where?

ANNE: Memory. It's not really a place. Not one you can point to, like on a map.

EMMETT: Is it Heaven?

ANNE: No, it's not Heaven. It's just . . . Memory. A magical place where you can look into the past, be in the present, and know everything that's happened since . . .

EMMETT: There's no time here?

ANNE: No. There's no clock or calendar here. Only truth. And the truth is . . . well, timeless.

EMMETT: I don't understand what I'm doing here . . . How do I get out?

ANNE: The same way you got in.

EMMETT: I don't get it.

ANNE: *(Points to her head)* Someone must have thought about you. "Cogito ergo sum."

EMMETT: What are you talking about?

ANNE: *(Proudly)* It's Latin.

EMMETT: You showing off?

ANNE: No. It just popped into my head. A philosopher once said, "I think, therefore I am."

EMMETT: So, I don't think, and therefore I'm not?"

ANNE: No. Come on. Stop being so—

EMMETT: Difficult?

ANNE: What I meant was that we're all here together in the darkness and alone at the same time until we're pulled into the light, until we're remembered . . .

EMMETT: By who?

ANNE: By whom.

EMMETT: *(Sarcastically)* Okay, by *whom*?

ANNE: I don't know. It could be anyone. But something happened to cause someone to think about you, to remember you, and therefore you are! You exist. Well, that is, as long as they keep thinking about you, remembering you.

EMMETT: What happens when they stop? Do I get out of here?

ANNE: You'll disappear. Just like chalk being erased from a blackboard. As if you never lived at all.

EMMETT: I don't get to choose whether I stay or go?

ANNE: No, not any more than I do.

EMMETT: How will I know when they'll let me leave?

ANNE: The lights start to flicker, then dim, then . . . it's back to darkness.

Emmett: How come you know so much about this place?

Anne: Maybe because I've been here longer . . . and been remembered by a lot more people.

Emmett: You said you had no choice either about staying or leaving . . . Do you want to stay here?

Anne: Yes. I want to stay here as long as possible. I want people to remember me . . . forever.

Emmett: I still don't understand why anyone would think of us here . . . together. I mean, it's hard to imagine . . .

Anne: Imagine! That's it. Someone imagined us together, that we were connected in some way.

Emmett: Come on. You're a white girl. I'm a Black boy. What do we have in common?

Anne: I don't know. Maybe someone felt we needed to talk about our lives, how we got here . . . and why. Maybe because of what happened to us when we were so young.

There's a reason . . . All I know is that we probably don't have much time together. Memory fades. It doesn't last very long.

Emmett: You said it was timeless here.

Anne: I said the truth was timeless, not Memory. So why don't we start over. My name's Anne. Anne Frank. And you are?

Emmett: *(A beat)* Emmett . . . Emmett Till.

(*Anne offers to shake hands, but Emmett pulls back, looks down.*)

Anne: Why do you keep looking away? Are you afraid of me?

Emmett: I'm not afraid of anybody.

ANNE: Then why do—

EMMETT: Rules. I'm not supposed to—

ANNE: There are no rules here. You're totally free. *(She pirouettes around the stage.)* I just think that you're shy around girls.

EMMETT: I have plenty of girlfriends.

ANNE: *(Playfully)* You're too young.

EMMETT: *(Pulls out his wallet)* I got a picture of one of them.

ANNE: *(Laughs sarcastically)* She's not your girlfriend. She's a movie star. That's Hedy Lamarr. I know all of the stars.

EMMETT: *(Embarrassed)* I have others. Real ones.

ANNE: Oh, sure you do. Hah!

(EMMETT decides to change the subject; he reaches over to pick up several sheets of paper on the floor and glances at them.)

ANNE: Hey! Stop! Don't touch those! They're personal. You have no right to read—

EMMETT: Okay. Here. Don't mean nothin' to me . . . I didn't read them. I don't care what's in them.

ANNE: They're special to me. I was writing—

EMMETT: Looked real special on the floor.

ANNE: And you came crashing in and spoiled everything.

EMMETT: I wasn't trying to crash in.

ANNE: Well, I certainly didn't invite you here. You really shouldn't be here. You need to go.

EMMETT: And then be forgotten?

ANNE: I'm sorry. I know it's not up to you to leave. I didn't mean . . .

EMMETT: To be mean?

ANNE: No. It's just that there's this dream that I had. I've been trying to put it into words exactly as it happened. Every time I get close, it keeps eluding me, slipping away. I just about had it when you . . . interrupted me.

EMMETT: What's so important about a dream? Can't you just have another one?

ANNE: No. Not like this one. It . . .

EMMETT: So, who's Kitty?

ANNE: Hey, I thought you said you weren't reading them. *(Mockingly)* "Don't mean nothin' to me."

EMMETT: I wasn't reading them. Just saw the name Kitty.

ANNE: She's my best friend.

EMMETT: Where is she?

ANNE: In my diary.

EMMETT: Huh?

ANNE: Kitty was the one person I used to tell all my secrets to, the one person who wouldn't judge or criticize me. Or betray my thoughts or moods. I could tell her everything and not have to pretend I was happy when I was miserable or . . .

EMMETT: Was she a real person?

ANNE: Real enough to me.

EMMETT: How come you called her Kitty?

ANNE: After my beautiful cat, Moortje.

EMMETT: You had a cat named Moor . . . Moort . . .

ANNE: Moortje.

EMMETT: Whatever happened to Moort . . . Moor— yo cat?

ANNE: I don't know. I had to leave her behind once we were forced to hide from the Nazis . . . It's a long story.

EMMETT: That's okay. Just tell me as much as you can.

ANNE: I was born in Germany. It was a beautiful country. Rolling hills, fields of flowers. We had a lovely home there. It was filled with books and music. My father loved to read.

(The lights come up on OTTO, who has been standing onstage in the shadows.)

OTTO: I wanted Anne and Margot to study all of the great minds. I used to read to them in German, French, English . . .

EMMETT: Sounds like you had a pretty nice life.

ANNE: Oh, yes. It was wonderful . . . until Hitler and the Nazis came to power. They turned everyone against us.

EMMETT: Us?

ANNE: Those of us who were Jewish.

EMMETT: How come? What did you do?

OTTO: We didn't *do* anything!

EMMETT: Then why did the Nazis turn the German people against you?

ANNE: Because we were *Jewish*! "Die Juden sind unser Unglück."

EMMETT: Dee what?

ANNE: It's German. It meant, "All our misfortunes are the fault of the Jews!" It was written on all the posters, in all the papers.

EMMETT: Misfortunes? I'd always heard that Jewish people were the "chosen people." Never knew what it meant, but it sounded like something good, something special.

OTTO: We were chosen, all right . . . for special persecution, special suffering. Made slaves in Egypt. Burned at the stake during the Spanish Inquisition.

ANNE: Then the Nazis decided that *they* had a "*Final* Solution" for us . . . the extermination of every Jew.

EMMETT: I don't understand. What made the Nazis hate you?

ANNE: Why are people always asking us to explain the hatred of others? Why don't you ask the Nazis?

EMMETT: I don't see any Nazis around. I was just asking.

ANNE: You really don't know?

EMMETT: No.

ANNE: They blamed us for everything . . . the economy, unemployment, social unrest . . . They even said that we were the reason they lost the First World War!

EMMETT: Far as I know, no one in Chicago ever blamed the Jewish people for anything or wanted to hurt them. The Jewish people were real friendly to us. They had stores in our neighborhood.

Abe Meltzer owned a butcher shop my momma used to go to. He always double ground the hamburger meat for her. He was real nice to me too . . . To me, Jewish people were just . . . white people. Being Jewish mean something else?

ANNE: No . . . I mean . . . well, yes. Our religion is different. We have a different history, culture, tradition . . . But I think being Jewish is really all about . . . morality. Living a moral life according to God's law as written in the Torah.

EMMETT: Aren't all religions about morality . . . knowing right from wrong? You saying Jewish religion's more moral?

ANNE: No. No. Not *more* moral. Our religion . . . traditions are not better, just . . . different. Whenever people start to think they're better or superior, that's when you get a Hitler. He believed the Aryans were superior—the "master race."

EMMETT: Sounds real familiar. In America, white people thought they were superior too. Especially those living down South. And they treated Black folks, well . . . real bad. My mother was worried about me when I traveled down there. I had a spirit, real spunk, you know? And I think it scared her.

(MAMIE *appears from the shadows.*)

MAMIE: Of course it scared me. You had no idea what white people down there were capable of doing! You never saw a Black man or woman swinging from a tree. Never saw the night riders in their hoods run their horses up on your porch, threatening to set your house on fire or shoot a gun through the doors. You never saw the face of hate . . .

ANNE: I think Hitler hated us because of our success. We excelled in everything. Medicine. Music. Science. Art. Business. Law. And because we were successful, because we were different and didn't want or need to be like the other Germans, they wanted to take everything we had . . . take all of us away.

EMMETT: Couldn't you stop being different? Be just like the rest of the Germans?

ANNE: Some did. But most of us couldn't. Or wouldn't. For my family, for me, the answer was no. We were Germans, but we were Jews first. We were Jews even before we believed in God. We couldn't stop being Jewish . . . any more than you can stop being . . . Black.

EMMETT: So, your religion is like . . . a race?

ANNE: No. Not exactly.

EMMETT: But you just said—

ANNE: I was trying to make a point . . . Never mind.

EMMETT: Okay, if you couldn't change being Jewish, why didn't you just leave Germany?

ANNE: We did. We tried to go to America, but President Roosevelt refused us. I guess there were too many ahead of us who wanted to do the same thing.

EMMETT: Couldn't you go somewhere else?

ANNE: Yes, but most countries wouldn't let us in. There was a German ship, the MS *St. Louis* . . . It had more than nine hundred Jewish passengers on board trying to immigrate to Cuba.

EMMETT: What happened to them?

ANNE: The Cubans let just a few people get off the ship. The rest had no place to go . . . They begged to land in America, but they were turned away. Because there was a law—a strict policy on admitting immigrants.

EMMETT: Where'd they go?

ANNE: Back to Europe, where many ended up in what Hitler called his "work camps." Then . . . there was no escape. The Nazis said that the only way out was . . . through the smoke stacks!

EMMETT: An American president treated white people like that?

ANNE: Yes, Emmett. It was shameful, unspeakable! He knew . . . everyone knew what the Nazis were doing. They just didn't care enough to stop them!

EMMETT: But our folks said that Roosevelt was a good man, especially after Hoover. Hard to believe he would turn those people away . . . But you got out?

ANNE: Yes. To Holland.

EMMETT: Were you safe there?

ANNE: At first, but the Nazis kept invading country after country in Europe. Holland too. They started imposing restrictions on us . . . confined us to ghettos . . .

EMMETT: Oh, I know something about ghettos . . .

ANNE: We had to step off the sidewalks whenever the Nazis approached us. We were forbidden to look them in the eye.

EMMETT: Know something about that too.

ANNE: They made us wear patches on our clothes with the yellow Star of David on them.

EMMETT: Star of David?

ANNE: The symbol of Jewish people. Like the Cross for Christians. We had to wear the patches on the front and back of our clothes so they could see us coming and going.

EMMETT: We didn't have to wear any patches. Skin color was enough.

ANNE: When we could go to the movies, we had to sit way up in the balcony.

EMMETT: Us too. They called it the "crow's nest."

ANNE: Then they imposed a curfew on us so we couldn't even be on the streets at night!

EMMETT: There were lots of places we couldn't be out after dark either. They had "sundowner" rules for us too: "Don't be caught in town after sundown, boy."

(Yelling) "Boy, you hear me? I said, do you hear me, boy?"

ANNE: "You hear me, kike?"

EMMETT: Jigaboo!

ANNE: Hebe!

EMMETT: Darky!

ANNE: Hymie!

EMMETT: Spook!

ANNE: Hook nose!

EMMETT: Flat nose!

ANNE: Dirty Jew!

EMMETT: Coon!

ANNE: Christ killer!

EMMETT: Nigger!

ANNE: Nig—?

EMMETT: Stop. *You* can't say that . . .

ANNE: I didn't mean any—

EMMETT: White folks came up with all those names, but that was the one that hurt the most. We used to be called Negroes . . . another word for *Black*. Guess that sounded a little too respectable, too civilized. But

Nigger, well, it's like a thing, an animal, a monkey . . . which is pretty much how they thought of us. "Nigger" was the last name Black people heard when they were being lynched.

ANNE: Now that I know what it means, I don't like it.

EMMETT: I don't like it either.

ANNE: If I can't say it, then you shouldn't either . . . It's just that words have power. They create images and images can hurt. The Nazis had all those names for us too. They made horrible, grotesque drawings of us. Said we were subhuman. Said we were devils . . . even had horns growing out of our heads.

EMMETT: They gave us horns *and* tails.

ANNE: They put up cruel posters and pictures everywhere in Europe, and that was just the beginning. Then they started rounding us up, sending us to their camps on their trains. That's when we knew we had to hide. We had to move from our home in Holland into the attic of an office building. We hid there for two years in a place we called the Secret Annex . . .

EMMETT: For two years. What was that like?

ANNE: It was horrible.

EMMETT: You couldn't go out at all?

ANNE: No. Not ever . . . I missed the fresh air, riding my bicycle with the wind in my hair, the sunshine on my face . . . During the day, I could look out one window at the very top of the Annex, the one where no one could see in, and see that beautiful chestnut tree outside. It was so full of life and free. Being free, that was the most important thing for me . . . Sometimes at night, Peter and I would open the window and just stare at the stars . . .

Emmett: I liked looking at the stars too. Could pick out the Big Dipper, Little Dipper, Orion's Belt . . . Wait. You said *Peter*. You had a brother?

Anne: He wasn't my brother. Just the son of the family hiding out with us. We were just . . .

Emmett: Friends? Uh-huh . . . All that time in the attic?

Anne: *Annex*, not attic. Besides, it's none of your business.

Emmett: I was just—

Anne: Just what? Implying that we had . . .

Emmett: No. I thought you . . .

Anne: I don't like the way you think!

Emmett: Hey! Have it your way. I get it. Frankly, I don't give a—

Anne: You shouldn't talk to me that way.

Emmett: Man, you are . . .

Anne: What?

Emmett: Look, let's drop it. It's not worth talking about. Especially since you were the one who said we don't have much time here.

Anne: I'm sorry. It's just . . .

Emmett: What?

Anne: Never mind. Anyway, to answer your question, Peter had a crush on me. We didn't do anything. But my father said that I had the responsibility to pull back from Peter. Why me? Why wasn't it just as much Peter's responsibility to stop as mine? Always the double standard for me, as if I'm the one who caused all the trouble . . . Anyway, it was just as well. Peter really wasn't the boy for me. He was too boring and unambitious. He was just, well . . . there.

EMMETT: *(Mockingly)* Petah. Boring. Unambitious . . . Uh-huh . . . Listen, I really wasn't trying to be nosy about Petah . . . I just find it hard to understand being stuck anywhere for two years.

ANNE: It was more like a lifetime . . . You have no idea what it was like to live with eight scared people all crammed into a small place. There was no privacy. We couldn't move around, make any noises, or do anything that might let the Nazis know we were there. When someone got sick, we couldn't just call a doctor . . . It was maddening. It was like being in a tomb . . .

EMMETT: Sounds scary.

ANNE: We were terrified. Terrified that the Nazis, the Dutch police might hear our voices, our little fights and jealousies. People . . . even family—*especially family*—can be so petty and selfish at times . . . so . . . Except my father. Poppa was my favorite person in the whole world. I miss him most of all.

EMMETT: What about your mother? Don't you miss her?

ANNE: Yes, I do, but . . . I really didn't like her. There were times when I even hated her.

EMMETT: You hated your mother? Wow. My mother was my best friend! You hated your mother?

ANNE: She criticized me for everything . . . My older sister, Margot, was her favorite. She could do no wrong. But I was always the one Mother picked on. I could never do anything right. I could never be the person I really was.

Poppa was the only one who really understood me. He tried to hold everything together, but it was hard. We were always in each other's way. Each other's moods . . . Honestly, it was so . . . exasperating. The others didn't like it when I talked or when I said nothing. If I was tired, they said I was lazy. I could never be smart, just cunning or clever.

EMMETT: Well, if you—

ANNE: When I was serious, they thought I was joking. When I was joking, they thought I was serious. Everything I did seemed to antagonize them . . . They even called me a chatterbox!

EMMETT: No kidding!

ANNE: There were times when I wished I'd been born with a different personality.

EMMETT: But then you wouldn't have been you . . .

ANNE: Yes, but I—

EMMETT: I liked being me. Liked telling jokes all the time. Trying to make people laugh. Everyone thought I was pretty funny . . . Maybe that's the advantage of being an only child.

ANNE: And the advantage of not being stuffed in an attic.

EMMETT: You mean *Annex*?

ANNE: Touché.

EMMETT: Too . . . ?

ANNE: *Touch*é. It's French. It means "You got me." . . . Now I guess I'm showing off.

EMMETT: You don't have to impress me.

ANNE: It's . . . just that it was all so depressing . . . I used to find a place to go and write just so I could be alone and talk to—

EMMETT: *(Triumphantly)* Moortje! Kitty.

ANNE: Exactly. I still miss her. And I'm still mad.

EMMETT: How come?

ANNE: They let Peter keep his cat in the *Annex*. It was used to catch rats. It kept urinating everywhere. Do you know what cat urine smells like?

EMMETT: Nope.

ANNE: It smells like fear. The smell of fear was in our clothes, our hair, our hands. It was everywhere. In everything. We couldn't wash it away . . . Then the plumbing stopped. We were . . . trapped.

EMMETT: I never had to live cooped up like that!

OTTO: *(Appears from the shadows)*

Being "cooped up" was better than being captured. We knew what they were doing to our people. Taking them off to concentration camps in railroad cars . . . packed in like cattle. When they arrived at the camps, they would separate everyone . . . mother from child, husband from wife, weak from strong, old from young. They counted and numbered everything: clothes, shoes, jewelry, people—especially people. They tattooed their arms with numbers . . . stripped them of anything they had left. Anything of value . . . They pulled off all their wedding bands and carted them away in wheelbarrows . . .

ANNE: Even took the gold out of the teeth of the dead.

EMMETT: Really? Took gold from their teeth?

ANNE: There wasn't anything they wouldn't do . . . One of the first things they did was to cut off everyone's hair. Imagine cutting off the hair of the women and girls and using it as . . . mattress stuffing!

EMMETT: My momma always said that a woman's hair was her crowning glory. They used it for . . .

Anne: Mattress stuffing . . . They claimed it was for health reasons. Get rid of lice and things . . . It wasn't health. It was humiliation . . . make everyone just another number . . . Then there were the experiments . . . at Auschwitz. Josef Mengele . . . the "Angel of Death." He put people in pressure chambers to measure their tolerance for pain. Took twin children and drew blood from them until they died . . . He . . .

Emmett: I had no idea all that was going on . . . What the Nazis were doing to your people. When I was growing up, I got to see all those movies and newsreels about the war in Europe . . . American and British planes dropping bombs on German cities and soldiers.

I remember seeing the films of Jesse Owens kicking the Germans' butts during the '36 Olympics. Man, could he run! People said Hitler was so mad, he left the stadium. Wouldn't even shake Jesse's hand.

Anne: We had Gretel Bergmann! A high jumper. I swear she could jump over the moon! Hitler wouldn't let her compete just because she was Jewish!

Emmett: Guess they both showed Ole Hitler something about his "master race." . . . You know, Anne, maybe, like you said, there's a reason for us to be here talking. Maybe we got a whole lot in common . . . more than anybody ever thought about before.

I mean, the Nazis packed and shipped you off in trains? Well, white folks came to Africa, packed us in slave ships, and shipped us off to America. When we got here, they separated us, just like they did to you. Mothers from children, husbands from wives . . . And we got robbed too. Robbed of our names, family, language, freedom . . . everything.

They sold us off on auction blocks. Like . . . cattle! They wanted our free labor, to slave and work. Sometimes they tattooed and branded us, but, like I said, the color of our skin was brand enough . . .

You talked about gold! My people were the gold—black gold! And just like the Nazis did to your people, white folks did to us! Humiliated and dehumanized us. Said we were only three-fifths human . . . Even deer and rabbits had more rights than we did . . . There were limits on how many deer you could kill and when you could kill them. There was a fine to pay if you broke those rules. But, man, down South, it was always open season on us. They'd say, "We shoot rabbits, but we hang our Nig—" Sorry . . . "our Negroes."

ANNE: They could hang you?

EMMETT: Yeah. For any reason. Any season. Hang and mutilate us in front of mobs all dressed up in their Sunday best as if they were at a picnic. Part of the entertainment for the day. They would even bring their kids to teach them early that's the way to treat Negroes.

ANNE: They wanted their children to see that?

EMMETT: They sure did! But just killing us wasn't enough for them . . . They set us on fire, cut off our fingers one by one, our ears, our knuckles, other . . . body parts . . . Took them as souvenirs. Even put them in jars in the grocery store windows, like pickles . . . Nazis used your hair to stuff mattresses . . . well, all those church-going white folks used to take pieces of our hair and tape them onto pictures of the lynchings and mail them to their friends just to prove they were there.

You talked about experiments. For forty years, our government used Black men to test how disease affected them when it went untreated . . .

ANNE: Oh, Emmett! I thought we were the only ones who had been treated like that . . . Why would they do this to you?

EMMETT: Different color skin, I guess.

ANNE: Your skin . . . It's darker. Different, but . . . there has to be more to it than color. Come on, let's compare—

EMMETT: Uh-uh.

ANNE: What's wrong?

EMMETT: That's how I got into trouble.

ANNE: There's no trouble here.

EMMETT: Maybe not but . . . What's wrong with your arm?

ANNE: Nothing.

EMMETT: Anne, were you ever . . . tattooed? Did they hurt you? . . . I heard about a man named Frank . . . down in Georgia.

ANNE: Leo . . .

EMMETT: Was he a relative?

ANNE: No. *Frank* is a pretty common name. It's a real shame what happened to him . . . But let's talk about you, Emmett. I still don't understand why whites hated you.

EMMETT: So now you want me to explain why we were hated? Why don't—

ANNE: No, well, I mean . . .

EMMETT: They didn't hate us in the beginning. They just wanted to use us. Make us do all the work for them for nothing. Later, they feared us . . . saw how strong we were. They felt weak . . . inferior physically . . . So they had to hold us down. Down and back. Prevented us from learning to read or write and then claimed we were just dumb when we couldn't read or write.

ANNE: So they could keep you down. Dominate you!

EMMETT: Exactly! Keep us in our place.

ANNE: The Nazis feared us too, but since they couldn't dominate us, they wanted to destroy us.

EMMETT: Destroy you. Dominate us.

ANNE: You know, it's so . . . so absurd. I'm white and Jewish . . .

EMMETT: Yeah. And I'm Black and Christian . . .

ANNE: But they came for both of us . . . It wasn't about religion or color . . . Like you said, it was fear.

EMMETT: But why . . . why do people have to fear and hate whatever or whoever is different?

ANNE: Maybe it's just that everyone needs to think they're better than someone else, and when they realize they're not . . .

EMMETT: Tell you the truth . . . the more I think about it, this whole thing about fear is just an excuse for hate. I mean, if someone says they acted out of fear, they think that makes it more acceptable. They just don't want to admit it, but it's really all about hate.

ANNE: But I could never understand it . . . Everyone loved our music, our art, our dedication to science, medicine, law. We've given so much to the world. I always wondered, what would the world be like without us? Albert Einstein, Marc Chagall, Emma Lazarus, George and Ira Gershwin, Vladimir Horowitz, Justice Louis Brandeis . . . I can count hundreds . . . Jonas Salk, the doctor who discovered the vaccine for polio . . .

EMMETT: Salk? Heard about him all right. Guess he came a little late for me . . .

ANNE: What do you mean "late for you"?

EMMETT: I had polio when I was six years old. It affected my speech somehow... made me stutter.

ANNE: I didn't know polio could cause stuttering... But you're okay now?

EMMETT: It usually happens when I'm nervous... But here in Memory, everything seems to be okay...

Anne, what you said about what Jewish people have given the world? I was just thinking... what would America—the world, for that matter—be like without our free labor, our music, art, science... Frederick Douglass, George Washington Carver, Dr. Charles Drew, W. E. B. Du Bois, Justice Thurgood Marshall, Duke Ellington... I mean *the* Duke Ellington! Ida B. Wells, Paul Robeson...

It's really sick. America was built on our backs. But once we started to resist... demand equal rights, they said, "If you Negroes don't like the way we do things around here, go back to Africa!"

ANNE: The Nazis felt the same way about us, Emmett, but they couldn't send us anywhere. We didn't have a place to go to back to then.

EMMETT: You said *then*. But now?

ANNE: Now we have our own country. A place that's ours. The land God promised us.

EMMETT: After all that's happened, you still believe? In God?

ANNE: Yes! It's important to have something to believe in, to have a religion. It doesn't matter what religion... Jewish, Christian, as long as you believe...

EMMETT: Did Hitler believe? Did he have a religion?

ANNE: He was Catholic, but the only thing he practiced was Nazism . . .

EMMETT: But you still have faith?

ANNE: I'm not naive, if that's what you're implying. I know the world's not filled with jelly beans and cotton candy!

EMMETT: *(Jokingly)* Careful now, Anne, when you talk about cotton.

ANNE: Despair—that's the alternative, isn't it? Well, not for me. I still believe that mankind is basically good.

EMMETT: Basically good? Wars, famine, slaughter . . .

ANNE: Sure, there's all of that. But there are people who perform a thousand acts of kindness every day . . . who—

EMMETT: Whooee! Must have missed some of those folks in Mississippi!

ANNE: People are born good . . . When I look into a baby's eyes, I see innocence . . . yes, goodness.

EMMETT: What did you see in the eyes of the Nazis?

ANNE: Hate . . . Evil.

EMMETT: That's my point. There's just as much hate and evil as there is goodness. Maybe more . . . There's something I never understood. I mean, I always praised God. I prayed to Him. I promised to be good. And I was . . . mostly . . . But when I needed Him most, He didn't hear me . . .

ANNE: I prayed too . . . But I think that we may be asking too much. I mean, to think that God has to listen to hundreds of millions of us every moment.

EMMETT: But what's a God for if He doesn't listen or hear us when we really need Him?

ANNE: I'm not sure if God is a He or a She for that matter . . .

EMMETT: Oh, man . . .

ANNE: I think God is a . . . a moral force, a power that creates, gives life.

EMMETT: And then what? Moves on to some other planet? We had landlords like that. Absentee landlords. Never made any repairs. Just let things go.

ANNE: It's complicated, Emmett. I don't have all the answers.

EMMETT: If God is all-perfect, how come He created something so imperfect? How could He allow such evil to—

ANNE: I don't know. Sometimes I wonder whether evil is just some dark force floating around the universe, waiting to enter the human heart. To feed off it and grow stronger with every act of cruelty.

EMMETT: Evil needs us to live?

ANNE: Maybe it's we who need evil so that we can know kindness, decency. Maybe we could never appreciate perfection if everything were already perfect.

EMMETT: Now that's heavy; must be one of those philosophers you talk about. No day without night, no love without hate . . . So, hate and murder are always going to be with us or them?

ANNE: No, they don't have to be out there hating. Not always. Not if people are willing to recognize evil before it becomes too strong . . . I still believe that the good people in the world will stop the hatred, the killing . . .

EMMETT: Oh, please . . .

Anne: There were times when I felt the same way, Emmett, but I realized that through all our suffering, we came out stronger. It made us survivors. We held onto our faith, our tradition. That's how we survived over the centuries.

Mamie: *(Appears from the shadows)* Our traditions were ripped away from us on those slave ships and auction blocks. You have no idea how slavery really messed with us. Divided us from each other and then against each other. Field slaves against house slaves . . . light skin against dark skin . . . It's all so . . . so . . .

Anne: But things got better for you, didn't they?

Emmett: I don't know. Everything is dark after . . .

Anne: After what?

Emmett: After what happened to me.

Anne: What happened? Tell me.

Emmett: No. No. I don't want to talk about it . . . It's too hard.

Anne: You have to try.

(There is a long pause between them.)

I like your hat, Emmett. Do you always wear it?

Emmett: I've always liked wearing a hat. I guess from the time I was four or five. It made me feel older, like a man. I was always in a hurry to grow up. The future seemed so far off. Never thought that it would come so fast . . . Never thought I'd have to leave so soon.

Anne: Emmett, you still haven't told me what happened to you. You need to talk about it.

Emmett: I told you, I don't want to talk about it!

ANNE: But you have to . . . Tell me. What are you thinking?

EMMETT: So many things . . . I'm thinking about my father. He was in Europe during the war. He died over there. The Army sent his ring to my mother. Nothing else. Nothing about how he died. Telegram just said, "Willful misconduct." Black soldiers fought against Hitler too, you know. Hollywood never made many movies about them. They helped defeat the Nazis, but the US government ended up treating German prisoners of war better than us . . .

ANNE: You're not serious!

EMMETT: Oh, yes, I am. German prisoners could eat and drink in our officer clubs, and Black officers were arrested and tossed in jail for demanding the same rights. Even court-martialed! Baseball great Jackie Robinson was one of them . . . The fact that Blacks could fight and die for America but couldn't wear their uniforms in public down South when they came home for fear of being beaten or lynched . . . Any white man, even a Nazi, was considered better than a Nigger . . . even one fighting for America! . . .

ANNE: Emmett, you're angry. I understand that . . . But anger only eats away inside. It doesn't change anything. Just remember, while you were trying to get into the officer clubs, we were trying to stay out of the ovens!

EMMETT: You're right. Anger doesn't change anything. Just scares people whenever we let the rage out. We couldn't even talk about racism . . . not if we wanted to get ahead. "Be a good boy. Don't cha' go being an angry Nigger now!"

ANNE: That's not what I meant! It's just that I don't understand why you can't see how things have gotten so much better. All I'm saying is that progress has been made. Why can't you accept that?

EMMETT: Real easy for you to talk about acceptance.

ANNE: Meaning what?

EMMETT: Meaning things are easier for you.

ANNE: Things weren't so easy for me in Germany.

EMMETT: Maybe not. But you'd have it made in the shade in America. All you'd have to do is change your name, change your hair and you could pass . . . In America, your religion isn't as important as what color you are. It only matters if you're white. And in America, your people get to be white!

ANNE: So, you're comparing who suffered more?

EMMETT: No, I'm not saying that. We both ended up dead. I'm just saying . . . that in America, color is a prison. We can never escape it. But if you're white, you're alright, and if you're Black, get back.

(*There is another long pause between them.*)

MAMIE: (*Appears onstage, singing from a Langston Hughes poem*)

Oh, what sorrow

Oh, what pity

Oh, what pain

That tears and blood

Should mix like rain

And terror come again . . .

EMMETT: I was living in Chicago. It was the summer of 1955. I went to visit my uncle and cousins in Mississippi . . .

MAMIE: And terror come again . . . to Mississippi!

(MAMIE *leaves the stage.*)

EMMETT: They were living and working there on a big plantation... My momma didn't want me to go.

ANNE: Why not?

EMMETT: Said it was too dangerous for me. That I wasn't used to all the rules down there.

OTTO: *(Voice offstage)* You have to know the rules.

ANNE: Rules?

EMMETT: Just like the Nazis had rules for you, the white man had rules for us. Momma warned me to be sure to—

MAMIE: —Mind your manners.

EMMETT: And be careful when it came to white folks. Not to look them in the eye. Be sure to call them sir and ma'am. Step off the sidewalk when a white person passed—especially a white woman... My cousins told me I had to be afraid... shuffle and scrape. Look like a "happy Negro," just as if we were on a plantation serving the "Massa." "Yassa. I's just an Uncle Tom." *(Does a little foot shuffle)*

Well, in Chicago we didn't have to do any of that stuff, and I was going to show my cousins that I was from the North and I wasn't afraid of anything.

ANNE: What, Emmett? What did you do?

EMMETT: I whistled...

ANNE: That's it? You whistled?

EMMETT: Yeah... at a white woman.

ANNE: Emmett, didn't you know it—

Emmett: I didn't mean any harm. I was just playing around, showing off... and it cost me my life...

(A beat)

I can't go back there. It's too... painful. I want to forget.

Anne: No, you can't forget. You have to tell what happened.

Emmett: *(A beat)* When I whistled at her, she just pointed a finger at me. My cousins scattered and ran for the car. They knew we were in trouble. They were so scared, they didn't say a word all the way home. None of us could sleep that night. The next day, nothing happened, so we thought everything was okay.

But a couple of nights later, some men came looking for me at my Uncle Mose's place. Took me to an old barn. Said they were going to teach me a lesson. Some lesson. Took an ax to me... gouged out one of my eyes, blinded me in the other... Momma!

My eye sockets feel like red-hot coals have been poured into them. I fall to my knees screaming... Everything is spinning around in my head. I can't breathe... The pain is so great, I think my whole body is on fire. I can't see them, can't tell where they are going to hit me again. Even though I'm scared and hurtin', I don't back down. I keep swinging my arms trying to fight back. Just makes them madder.

All the time, I know I'm dying. Things flashing through my mind. No more pranks, playing baseball, jumping in swimming holes, no more doo-woppin' and singing with my cousins. No more sweet hugs from my momma... Finally, they tie a big cotton-gin fan around me, shoot me in the head... *(The sound of a loud gunshot rings out.)* ... and throw me in the Tallahatchie River. Everything starts going blank... The last thing I can hear is them laughing and my body splashing in the water...

Funny, all the time they were beatin' and cuttin' me up, scared as I was I kept hoping that no one would ever find my body. All I could think of was what would happen to my momma if she ever saw what they had done to me. I could bear the dying easier than the thought of her crying...

(MAMIE *reappears onstage, dressed in a black dress and a small black hat.*)

MAMIE: They found my son's body floating in the river a couple of days later. They were about to bury him in Mississippi. No notice, no ceremony, no witnesses.

But I got a court order to have him brought back to me in Chicago. They had locked the casket and told the sheriff in Chicago that it was under Mississippi's State Seal and couldn't be opened. I was havin' none of that.

I told the sheriff to give me *(Shouts)* a hammer! Nothing was going to stop me from seeing what they had done to my little boy... The odor coming from the casket was so powerful, you could smell it a block away. The stink was like—well, like the devil's own breath. But I didn't care... I wasn't going to pour perfume to cover the stench of their hate...

I walked along the full length of the casket, beginning with his feet, and touched him all the way to his... face. Bo was beaten so bad, the only way I could tell it was him was because he was wearing his father's silver ring that had his initials on it—L. T., Louis Till. It broke my heart to . . . to see what they had done to my only child . . .

I knew that Bo wouldn't have wanted anybody, especially me, to see him looking like that. But I prayed on it all night long and just decided that I was going to tie the shame of his murder right around the necks of the cowards who murdered my beautiful boy.

(The hymn "Swing Low, Sweet Chariot" begins to play.)

At the funeral, I made sure the casket was open, the lid up! I wanted the world to see what they'd done to Bo . . . what they do to us . . .

ANNE: Oh, Emmett! It's horrible! . . . I'm so sorry. Was . . . was anything done to those men for what they did to you?

(J. W. MILAM enters the stage, dressed in a white T-shirt and jeans.)

J. W. MILAM: Well, what else could we do?

EMMETT: Nothing.

J. W. MILAM: I never hurt a nigger in my life. I like niggers—in their place.

EMMETT: Nothing happened.

J. W. MILAM: I know how to work 'em. But I just decided it was time a few people got put on notice. As long as I live and can do anything about it, niggers going to stay in their place. Niggers ain't going to vote where I live. If they did, they'd control the government. They ain't gonna go to school with my kids. And when a nigger gets close to mentioning sex with a white woman, he's tired o' livin'. I'm likely to kill him . . . I just made up my mind. "Chicago boy," I said,

"I'm tired of 'em sending your kind down here to stir up trouble. Goddamn you, I'm going to make an example of you—just so everybody can know how me and my folks stand."*

MAMIE: After the trial, the murderers gave an interview to *Look* magazine.

EMMETT: They got paid four thousand dollars for that interview!

MAMIE: And laughed how they got away with what they did—

EMMETT: To me.

MAMIE: To my Bo.

J. W. MILAM: *(Laughs)* Not guilty!

MAMIE: I will spend the rest of my life making sure no one will ever forget Emmett Till. And *Jet* magazine made sure of it. Put the photograph of how Bo looked in that casket in the magazine.

EMMETT: Word was that the photograph went worldwide. Even made news in a German newspaper. Headline read, "IN AMERICA, A NEGRO'S LIFE ISN'T WORTH A WHISTLE!"

They got that pretty much right.

ANNE: In America you can confess to murder and still go free? That's not justice!

EMMETT: Black man get justice in Mississippi? In America? If you're white, you bet . . . Oh, they held a phony trial. The defense attorney told the all-white jury that "Your ancestors would roll over in their graves if you ever convicted a white man for killing a *nigger*." Took the

---

*William Bradford Huie, "The Shocking Story of Approved Killing in Mississippi," *Look* 20, no. 2 (January 1956): 46–48, 50.

jury just about an hour—enough time for lunch— and they came back and acquitted the men who murdered me.

I'm real proud of my Uncle Mose, though. He stood up in a Southern court and pointed out those crackers who came for me that night. Took real courage for him to do that. He left town right afterward and headed for Chicago . . . He knew they'd kill him if he stayed around . . .

ANNE: Emmett, maybe you should have listened to your mother and your cousins. I mean you could still be alive today if—

EMMETT: If I'd what? Lived by the white man's rules?

MAMIE: Don't say anything . . .

EMMETT: Jumping off sidewalks to let white folks pass?

MAMIE: Just look down.

EMMETT: Licking their boots along the way?

ANNE: But you knew your life was worth more than a whistle.

MAMIE: You don't just look down . . .

ANNE: You . . .

MAMIE: Cross the street.

OTTO: *(Voice offstage)* You know the rules.

EMMETT: I know the rules, Momma!

ANNE: But you knew your life was worth more than a whistle. You—

EMMETT: You don't get it! It wasn't about the damn whistle! It was about hate! They hated me . . . just for being Black. They were looking for any excuse to beat me, kill me.

ANNE: But you knew what they would do if . . . they caught you . . .

EMMETT: So . . . I should have stayed silent?

(A beat)

Your silence didn't save you.

ANNE: *(Furious)* Now *you* don't get it! It was different for us. It's unfair for you to try and judge us . . . How dare you? You weren't there! You couldn't see what it was like—

EMMETT: But you judged me.

ANNE: I wasn't judging you.

EMMETT: But you must have known what would happen if—

ANNE: Of course we knew! We weren't stupid! Yes, we were afraid, but we didn't just run out into the streets, throw our hands up, and surrender. Some had the chance to escape, to survive in the woods. But those of us in the city were trapped. We had no way out, but we held onto hope . . . and dreams . . .

ANNE and EMMETT: *(Together)* Dreams . . .

ANNE: Emmett, I got it! I got it!

EMMETT: What?

ANNE: It's that dream I was trying to remember when you came here . . . I dreamed that a beautiful bird somehow had slipped into our Annex and had become trapped there. It kept crashing against the walls, falling to the floor, breaking its wings, but it wouldn't give up trying to fly free. There were other times when I . . . just . . . closed my eyes and imagined dark, murderous clouds all around us. But just above my head was a patch of blue sky. It was the only thing that gave me hope. Hope that the war would end and that we'd all be safe . . . free of the fear that filled every minute of our lives.

I remember the day when they came for us. Someone told them where we were hiding. We could hear those awful sirens in the distance. They grew louder and closer, and we knew we were in trouble.

We could hear shouting in the street, the sound of footsteps, then the tapping on the walls as they tried to find the hidden door to the Annex . . . Everyone was afraid to breathe . . . afraid they'd hear our slightest whimper . . . I held my breath until I was sure I was turning blue . . .

The tapping turned to thumping, the thumping to pounding . . . the sound of people on the stairs, suddenly a loud bang, and they were in. The Dutch police. They were hostile, smug, like hunters get when they've captured their prey. Mother nearly fainted. Margot went blank. Everything seemed to be suspended . . . a bad dream . . . I simply started to breathe again. The hiding was over. In a strange way, it was a relief. We had gone from being hidden to helpless to captured to . . .

I still find it hard to think about how the Nazis treated everyone. First at Westerbork, then Auschwitz, then Bergen-Belsen . . . Old faces, scared faces, puzzled faces. Somehow Margot and I were herded into the same group. Mother into another one, and Poppa . . . where did they take him? Auschwitz, I think, but I never saw him again . . .

(OTTO reappears onstage. He is dressed in a shabby prisoner's garment.)

OTTO: I've asked myself a thousand times: Why didn't I try to leave Europe sooner? I heard the echo of goose steps on the cobblestones. I knew what that sound meant. We Jews have heard the sound of hate coming so many times before. But I thought maybe this time was different. That there were places we could go . . . places that were safe . . .

How was I to know that France, Holland—all the others would fall so quickly? That America would not care or come soon enough? . . .

I knew that Hitler was a madman and that nothing straight could ever come from crooked wood. But who knew how much evil was carved in the twisted cross of the Nazis? The *Hakenkreuz*.

Who knew? Who knew? . . .

ANNE: It was all so surreal.

OTTO: The summer heat cooled to autumn; the air became colder.

ANNE: Winter was so bitter . . .

OTTO: We were hungry all the time, and sometimes we had to fight like animals for a scrap of food . . .

ANNE: Margot grew weaker . . .

OTTO: Quieter . . .

ANNE: More distant.

OTTO: All of us were starving.

ANNE: But I was in denial that she was starving to death . . . I became the older sister and gave her my food. I was determined to keep her alive. She was my only link to all that had been so beautiful in the past. She kept growing weaker, but the guards just kept giving us more work.

OTTO: We could see the Nazi soldiers smoking, laughing, joking, treating us like vermin, not human. They performed all kinds of cruel experiments . . . torture, executions, gassings, and . . . I'll never forget the smell of smoke, of burning souls . . .

ANNE: When Margot died, her body was dumped into a mass grave. I felt myself giving up. The only thing I had left was hope, and it was fading.

OTTO: Everyone had typhus . . . nausea, the scratching, the pain . . . But I held onto hope—

ANNE: I kept thinking of Poppa, how much I loved him, of how I used to write in my diary. I grew delirious, knew that I was dying, slipping away . . . Then I heard a soft tapping sound that soon became loud thumping. Was it the sound of the Dutch police coming for me again or just the last beats of my heart? Then the thumping turned to a flapping noise . . . The lights turned white, and suddenly I could see it was that sweet little bird I used to dream about. I wanted to set it free, to fly away with it into blue skies . . . Be Poppa's little girl again—

OTTO: To see my little girl—

ANNE: Riding my bicycle—

OTTO: Riding her bicycle—

ANNE: Studying my lessons—

OTTO: Studying her lessons—

ANNE: The flapping sound grew weaker, softer, then . . . nothing . . .

OTTO: Nothing, nothing, nothing . . .

(A beat)

God . . . where were you? My Anne, my Margot, my Edith, my dear family and all the millions of others. Did you not hear their screams? Were they not loud enough for your ears? Did you not see our suffering, the cruelty we had to endure? Or perhaps you could not see us because you are too far away? Or because you have no eyes. Answer me! Or maybe you are angry with us. Tell me, what did the innocent do, the children, the babies who were burned alive, thrown into the ovens of Auschwitz? Did they displease you? How were they unworthy of your love? Or did you let them die as a *sign* of your love? Is this how a God loves? Answer me!! Damn your silence. Maybe you can only hear me if I recite your prayer.

> Yis'ga'dal v'yis'kadash sh'may ra'bbo, b'olmo dee'vro chir'usay v'yamlich malchu'say b'chayaychon uv'yomay'chon uv'chayay d'chol bais Yisroel, ba'agolo u'viz'man koriv; v'imru Omein. Y'hay shmay rabbo m'vorach l'olam ul'olmay olmayo . . .

Still nothing. Still you are silent. God, this is your answer? Silence? . . . I know that you will not forgive my blasphemy, but I will not forget your silence . . .

Emmett: *(A beat)* Anne, I'm really sorry. I shouldn't have spoken to you that way.

Anne: You don't have to apologize . . . That's why we vowed to never allow anyone to try to destroy us. Why we say, "Remember! Never Again!"

To remind people the world over what we had to endure. Now it's a crime in some parts of Europe to promote anti-Semitism or say that the Holocaust never happened. You can go to jail just for saying that.

Emmett: You mean haters are prosecuted in Europe?

Anne: Exactly.

Emmett: But they're protected in America.

Anne: They can't be!

Emmett: The Ku Klux Klan and skinheads can march down any Main Street praising Hitler and have a police escort in the process . . .

Anne: Seriously?

EMMETT: Yes. They can wrap themselves in the American flag while saluting Hitler's and burn crosses knowing it's the symbol of white terrorism . . .

ANNE: That's terrible! Not only can't the haters deny what they did to us, but companies that profited during the Holocaust have to pay restitution to the survivors and their families. Make reparations.

EMMETT: Reparations? You get reparations?

ANNE: Absolutely. Under the law!

EMMETT: Under the law, we get nothing. Not a dime. Not a penny. White folks say slavery happened too long ago. They don't know who should pay. Or how much.

ANNE: They're wrong, Emmett. Time can't erase a crime against humanity. It's never too late for justice. It seems to me if scientists can figure out how long ago the Earth was created, they can figure out just how much is owed.

EMMETT: A few accountants would do. Those companies kept all sorts of records.

ANNE: Don't give up hope, Emmett. Remember how we did it.

EMMETT: Anne, you tell everybody to remember! Everybody tells us to forget!

"Stop playing the victim. Stop dragging the past around like some dead body in the cemetery. Bury it! It's history!" Black history, I guess. Not American history. We're always told to get over it! Just what's the *it* they want us to get over?

ANNE: I sympathize, Emmett, I really do . . .

EMMETT: But?

ANNE: But at some point, you have to . . .

EMMETT: To what? Get over it? My momma used to quote the Bible all the time, about the need for grace and forgiveness . . .

ANNE: But you didn't listen to her . . .

EMMETT: Let's not argue about that again.

ANNE: I'm not trying to argue. It's just that at some point, you've got to let the anger go . . .

EMMETT: Let it go where?

ANNE: It's just an expression!

EMMETT: Easy for you to say "let the anger go." The Europeans are trying to make up for what one man—Hitler—did to you . . . But who do we blame for four hundred years of hate? Washington? Jefferson? Johnson? Jackson? It was everyone . . . and no one . . . Like the police used to tell us, it all happened at the hands of "persons unknown" . . .

(A beat)

I wish I could let go of the rage. Anne, but I can't. I can never go back to being the carefree boy I once was . . . I can't forget that night . . . everything going dark . . .

ANNE: "The universe isn't dark enough to snuff out the light of a single candle." I don't remember who said that. But that's what I always try to do. In all the darkness, all the gloom, I light a candle . . . Inside, that is . . . I think of a candle flickering inside my mind. It makes me smile. Have hope. Believe that everything I've been through hasn't been a waste . . . You should try it, Emmett. Light a candle. Just one. Close your eyes and light it.

Emmett: I can't. Not yet. Maybe one day.

Anne: "One day" means never. You know that. Just try it.

(A beat)

Emmett, you had such a peaceful expression on your face when you closed your eyes. What were you thinking when you lit the candle?

Emmett: About my last birthday. I remember blowing out fourteen candles on my birthday cake. I made a wish . . . actually, two . . .

Anne: That's cheating.

Emmett: I know . . . I wished that one day I'd become a professional comedian, like Abbott and Costello or George Gobel. He was my favorite.

Anne: And the other wish?

Emmett: Oh, if I couldn't make people laugh, then I wanted to be a motorcycle policeman. I wanted to stop people from fighting. Be a peacemaker.

(Mamie appears, holding a birthday cake.)

(Otto appears, holding an armful of presents.)

Anne: I wanted so much to have a "sweet sixteen" birthday party, excited to open all the beautifully wrapped presents . . . my family and friends there celebrating. I would light all the candles and then, making a wish—just *one* wish—blow them all out.

Emmett: What would you have wished for?

Anne: You're not supposed to tell your wishes, or they won't come true . . . Of course, I guess it really doesn't matter anymore . . . But I would have wished to become a great writer, a poet and playwright . . . maybe even a movie star . . .

EMMETT: Hey! That's cheating.

ANNE: I know. Guess I would have cheated a little bit too . . . I think most of all what I wanted was to change the world. Make it a better place.

EMMETT: Looking back, if I'd lived, I know I would have done something big. I would have been somebody important . . . Maybe like Dr. King, marched for justice. That's what I would have wanted. Justice for Black people. Something we never had . . .

MAMIE: *(A beat)* But that's why I devoted the rest of my life to keeping the memory of you alive. To give meaning to your death . . . to inspire people to change things. You changed the course of American history, Emmett.

OTTO: And I did the same for you, Anne. Of the eight of us who were sent off to the concentration camps, I was the only one to survive. And when I discovered that the pages to your diary hadn't been destroyed or lost, I had them published so the world would know what life was like for you, for us . . . I wanted the everyone to see the truth.

ANNE: *(A beat)* Emmett, I was just thinking that your name, *Emet*, is the Hebrew word for "truth."

EMMETT: Really? Truth. Now how cool is that? And what about your name, Anne? What does it mean?

ANNE: In Hebrew, it means "favored grace."

EMMETT: So, you're grace, and I'm truth . . .

(A beat)

But . . . do you think any of it really matters to anyone? I mean, after all we've been through, we're just a moment in someone's mind? All they have to do is remember? That's it? They don't have to do anything? Take any action? We're stuck here between remembering history and repeating it?

ANNE: Until they change. Until the memory of the horrors of the past becomes so strong, so deeply embedded in their souls, that they say, "Enough. No more!" But memories fade quickly. I think it's happening already . . .

EMMETT: But if we exist because someone's thought about us, why can't it work the other way around?

ANNE: I'm not sure what you mean.

EMMETT: If people can imagine us together, like you said, pull us from the darkness into the light, why can't we ride that same beam of light right back to them? Why can't we tell them while they're thinking of us that they have to do something? To act! They have to stop being silent witnesses to crimes they know are going on, thinking they're safe!

ANNE: That's brilliant, Emmett. Yes, we can tell the world the truth— that the haters are still out there and that the good people in the world aren't standing up, aren't doing enough to stop them . . .

(The stage lights start to flicker.)

EMMETT: Anne, the lights . . . I think we need to hurry.

ANNE: *Tikkun olam.*

EMMETT: More Hebrew?

ANNE: Yes. It's from the Talmud. It means a moral obligation to repair the world.

EMMETT: That's what we can do. Join forces to repair the world!

ANNE: If we could show people how hate keeps changing its shape but always has the same message, the same goal—to divide people by race, religion, geography . . .

EMMETT: Divide . . . Dehumanize . . . Dominate . . . Destroy . . .

ANNE: If we can warn them, trap evil in a beam of light before it can slip back into the darkness . . . If we can touch their conscience, then just maybe we can save them.

EMMETT: At least some of them.

ANNE: Do you still want to leave Memory, Emmett?

EMMETT: No, I want to stay here, and just like you, Anne, I want be remembered . . . forever.

ANNE: Okay. Then let's go to the place where memories are kept and tell people they have to stop the hate.

EMMETT: Before it's too late.

ANNE: If they don't, we'll just be having this same conversation—

EMMETT: Over—

ANNE: And over—

EMMETT: And over . . .

(ANNE reaches out for EMMETT. He hesitates and then locks hands with her, and the two turn to walk upstage as the lights start to dim.

The stage goes completely dark.

The musical score of Anne & Emmett *begins to play.*

On the screen, a series of slides depicting the horrors of the Nazi genocidal persecution of European Jews and America's barbaric treatment of African Americans rolls, as the haunting musical theme of Anne & Emmett *continues.*

Photographs of Matthew Shepard, Trayvon Martin, Brandon Teena, Breonna Taylor, George Floyd, Jacob Blake, Merci Mack, Philando Castile . . . move silently across the screen.

The last photograph is of a burning cross that morphs into a swastika.

At the conclusion of the slide presentation, the words of Elie Wiesel, a prominent Holocaust survivor, appear on screen. We hear the same deep and sonorous voice that began the play recite Dr. Wiesel's admonition.)

VOICE-OVER: "To forget would be not only dangerous but offensive: to forget the dead would be akin to killing them a second time."*

THE END

---

*From the preface of Elie Wiesel, *Night*, trans. Marion Wiesel (New York: Hill and Wang, 2006).

AFTERWORD:
A TREE FOR EMMETT TILL

You got a right. I got a right. Everybody's got a right to the tree of life.

—Negro spiritual

Psychiatrist Viktor E. Frankl, in his classic memoir, *Man's Search For Meaning*, about his days in Nazi concentration camps, describes his conversation with a woman who was near death. She pointed to the branch of a chestnut tree that had two blossoms on it.

"This tree here is the only friend I have in my loneliness. . . . I often talk to the tree."

Frankl thought that the woman might be hallucinating. He asked if the tree responded.

"Yes. It said to me, 'I am here—I am here—I am life, eternal life.'"*

One of Anne Frank's singular joys during her confinement to the cramped quarters of the annex in Amsterdam was looking out a window that was hidden from the street below.

---

*Victor E. Frankl, *Man's Search for Meaning: An Introduction to Logotherapy*, trans. Ilse Lasch, pref. Gordon W. Allport, intro. Leslie D. Weatherhead (London: Hodder & Stoughton, 1946).

From there, she could see the blue sky, birds, and the beautiful chestnut tree when it was bare and when its limbs were bare and when they blossomed with leaves.

Anne wrote that she could not be sad as long as it existed.*

The tree that gave Anne such pleasure lived to be between 150 and 170 years old, finally succumbing to disease and the elements in 2010.

The Anne Frank House had arranged for dozens of saplings to be propagated before the tree's demise, with the intent of distributing them to schools, museums, and other organizations all over the world.†

One site selected was the West Front Lawn of the United States Capitol.‡

It occurred to me that a tree for Emmett Till would serve as a living monument to his life and to the history of African Americans in this country.

Through the office of the Architect of the Capitol, I learned that such a tribute would require the support of congressional leaders. I called upon Congressman John R. Lewis, one of the heroes of the modern Civil Rights Movement in the United States, and my husband, Bill, contacted Senator Susan Collins of Maine.

Both eagerly agreed to support my idea.

---

*The full passage reads, "Nearly every morning I go to the attic to blow the stuffy air out of my lungs. From my favorite spot on the floor I look up at the blue sky and the bare chestnut tree, on whose branches little raindrops shine, appearing like silver, and at the seagulls and other birds as they glide on the wind. As long as this exists, I thought, and I may live to see it, this sunshine, the cloudless skies, while this lasts I cannot be unhappy." From the entry dated February 23, 1944, in Anne Frank, *The Diary of a Young Girl*, trans. Barbara Mooyaart-Doubleday (Garden City, NY: Doubleday & Company, 1952).

†"The Chestnut Tree," Anne Frank House (website), n.d., https://www.annefrank.org/en/anne-frank/front-section/chestnut-tree/.

‡"The Sapling Project," The Anne Frank Center for Mutual Respect (website), n.d., https://www.annefrank.com/sapling-project.

Within a matter of weeks, a dedication ceremony was organized to take place on the Capitol Hill grounds.

It was a brisk autumn day, and the heavens opened up, sending an avalanche of rain onto the heads of all in attendance; but nothing could dampen my joy in that moment, when a dream was about to become a reality.

In fact, I took the rain as a ceremonial blessing, ordaining our presence, mission, and promise.

I didn't have prepared remarks to make. I simply spoke from my heart.

I wanted this tree for Emmett Till because his brutal murder is the symbol, a lasting and painful symbol, of what could happen to you, if you were Black in the twentieth century in this country, at the hands of Southern whites. I wanted the tree here on these grounds because Emmett Till's murder changed the course of this country's history. It changed me, a young Black girl, the same age as Emmett.

I was happy that summer until word came up from Mississippi. Then I was frightened and enraged—and now I have a purpose. I want people to remember Emmett Till—not only Emmett Till, but what happened to all the Emmett Tills. What happens to the Emmett Tills of today. They need to be remembered.

I wanted the tree to be in the shadow of the Capitol Dome because it was Emmett's and my ancestors as enslaved laborers that built that Dome and many of the buildings here in the nation's capitol.

Normally when we honor our nation's martyrs and icons, we cast them in stone and marble.

But for Emmett Till I wanted a living memorial. I wanted a tree. And some might say, *As an African American, you wanted a tree?*

Yes, because the tree has a painful history for us. Some trees in our dark past have borne strange fruit—Black men and women and children hanging from trees. Not all of us were thrown into rivers.

I want, when the generations to come, and this tree grows, when they pass by, I want them to remember, not to forget. And to take action.

As this little tree sinks its roots deep into the soil, I want it to grow wide and tall as American sycamores do. I want it to reach for the sun in the daytime, for the stars in the night, and inspire us to reach for our higher humanity.

Finally, Mr. Architect, I have to say how grateful I am that you picked an American sycamore tree. It's a beautiful tree. There's a larger one across the street. It's so significant in that its leaves are deciduous, and so is its bark.

Look at that full-grown tree. You'll see the bark is multicolored, much like we Africans are here in the diaspora.

We are black. We are brown. We are beige, cream, and we change colors. We grow tall and strong.

I'm very proud of that tree, and it reminds me of the song in *Pocahontas*: "Can you paint with all the colors of the wind?"

The lyrics are,

> How high will the Sycamore grow?
> If you cut it down, then you'll never know.

Emmett was cut down and will never know how tall he might've grown.[*]

---

[*]Janet Langhart Cohen, remarks made at the planting of the US Capitol Grounds Memorial Tree in honor of Emmett Till, Washington, D.C., November 17, 2014; from the personal library of the author.

SCORE FOR *ANNE & EMMETT*: A PIECE FOR STRING ORCHESTRA AND PIANO
JOSHUA COYNE (2009)

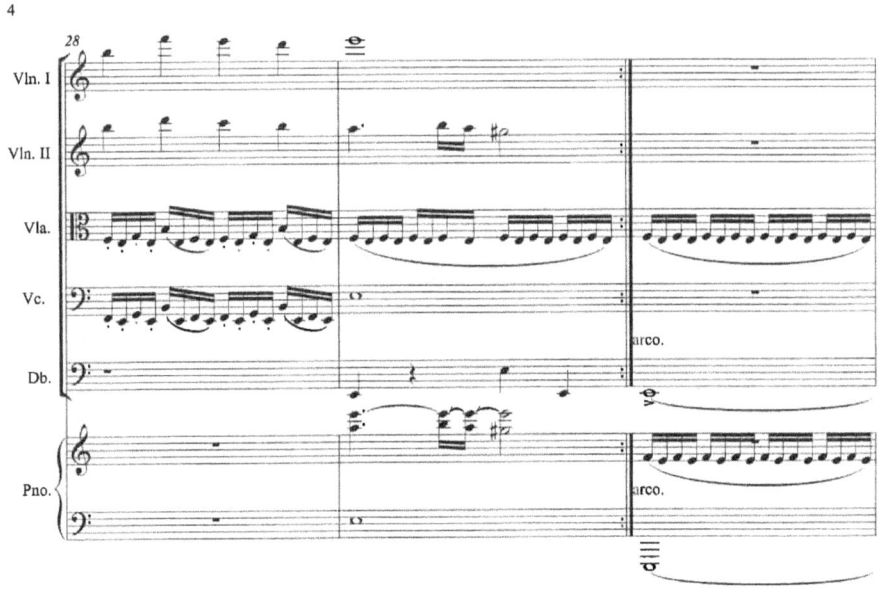

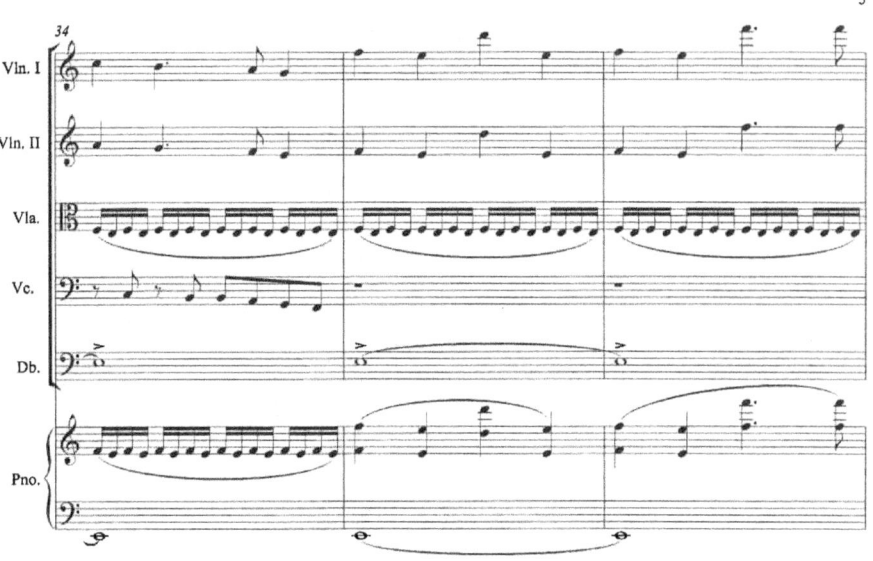

ACKNOWLEDGMENTS

I am deeply indebted to many friends and supporters, but special thanks go to

> Colette Phillips of Colette Phillips Communications, my friend of over thirty years, who enabled the play to stand on it's feet for the first time on the stage at her alma mater, Emerson College in Boston, Massachusetts.
>
> Cheryl Brown Henderson, daughter of Reverend Oliver Brown, namesake and a plaintiff in the historic US Supreme Court Decision Brown v. Board of Education, who invited me to bring *Anne & Emmett* to Topeka and Kansas City, Kansas, to commemorate the fifty-sixth anniversary of the decision.
>
> Eugene Robinson, Pulitzer Prize–winning journalist and television commentator, for his friendship and unflinching support in promoting justice for all.
>
> Avis Robinson, artist, educator, and philanthropist, for enabling me to realize my dream of having *Anne & Emmett* performed for middle-school students in the Arlington, Virginia, public-school system.
>
> Former NYPD Police Commissioner William Bratton, who invited the play to be performed for more than one thousand New York City Police Academy cadets.

Supreme Court Justice Ruth Bader Ginsburg, who hosted the play at the US Supreme Court before the National Association of Women Judges.

Chief Judge Anna Blackburne-Rigsby and Judge Betty Williams, who brought the play to the BMCC Tribeca Performing Arts Center.

Anna Deaveare Smith, brilliant actress, who performed the character of Mamie Till Mobley at the performance at the Harvard Club of New York City, where Vernon Jordan and Dr. Henry Kissinger served as sponsors.

Hank and Corinne Greenberg, whose unstinting friendship and support helped bring the play to young audiences throughout the country.

Academy Award–winning actor-director Michael Douglas, whose guidance over the years has been life-enhancing.

Lonnie Bunch, founding director of the National Museum of African American History and Culture, who, along with his wife, Maria, has attended virtually every performance of the play.

Westley Moore, warrior, scholar, and friend, who has lent his talents and those of his family, especially his mother, Joy, to the cause of promoting justice for all in America.

Sara J. Bloomfield, director of the United States Holocaust Memorial Museum, and Arthur Berger, public relations director, who were instrumental in preparing to bring *Anne & Emmett* to the museum.

Rabbi Shmuel Herzfeld of Ohev Sholom, The National Synagogue, in Washington, D.C., who has been my courageous spiritual guide.

Rabbi Paul F. Cohen of Temple Jeremiah in Northfield, Illinois, who hosted a sellout performance at the temple.

Rabbi M. Bruce Lustig of Washington Hebrew Congregation, who invited the play to be performed at the synagogue.

Operation Understanding DC, who sponsored the play at the Sixth & I synagogue in Washington, D.C.

The Black-Jewish Forum of Baltimore (BLEWS), who worked to bring the Jewish and Black communities together to fight racism and anti-Semitism.

Ron Himes, director of the Black Rep theater in Saint Louis, Missouri, whose stalwart support of *Anne & Emmett* helped it to the theater and classrooms in Saint Louis.

Ken Johnson, of the Duke Ellington School of the Arts, a great friend, who traveled the country, shepherding *Anne & Emmett* through its many performances.

Robin Harris, of the Duke Ellington School of Arts, who assisted in managing all of the logistics and mechanics involved in the play's may productions.

Maureen Monteiro, my longtime friend, who helped promote *Anne & Emmett* on the Web.

And Jamal Joseph, former Black Panther, now professor of film at Columbia University, who filmed and brilliantly edited a feature-length film of *Anne & Emmett*.

Finally, I have been blessed to have had the benefit of some of the finest directors in the country, including

Thomas W. Jones III, Atlanta, Georgia
Talvin Wilks, New York City
Hinton Battle, New York City

Ricardo Khan, founder of Crossroads Theatre, in New Brunswick, New Jersey
Ron Himes, The Black Rep, Saint Louis, Missouri
Robbie McCauley, performing arts professor, Emerson College, Boston, Massachusetts
Ari Roth, Theatre J, Washington, D.C.
Teddy Harrel, Jr., African American Cultural Arts Center, Miami, Florida
And Roy Lewis, Augusta Players, Atlanta, GA

Special recognition must go to

Tim Matheny, chairman, Department of Theatre and Communication, William Carey University, Hattiesburg, Mississippi
Tonya Hays, assistant professor of theatre performance, Mississippi State University, Starkville, Mississippi
And Edye Evans Hyde, Ebony Road Players, Grand Rapids, Michigan

All three directors determined that the *Anne & Emmett* "show must go on" even during the COVID-19 pandemic. They produced multiple performances virtually, and properly socially distanced. Three Cheers!

I am sincerely grateful to Jed Lyons, president and CEO of Rowman & Littlefield Publishing Group. While Jed was a student at Bowdoin College, he helped my husband Bill keep steady and safe on Bill's 600-mile walk across the state of Maine to win his first congressional race in 1972. Jed published *Love In Black And White: A Memoir of Race, Religion, and Romance*, which contained the initial draft of *Anne & Emmett*.

Jed assigned John Cerullo, senior executive editor and digital manager of Rowman & Littlefield to guide me, ever so patiently, through the long, production process. John, in turn, made sure that I had the assistance of his extraordinary editorial team, consisting of Naomi Minkoff, Carol Flannery, and Barbara Claire—who possess the eyes of eagles and can spot and swoop down on an error or omission with terrifying (to this author) speed.

Last, but always First among Equals, is my husband Bill—public servant, statesman and poet—for encouraging me to tell the story of why I wrote *Anne & Emmett*. Without his unwavering support to "stay the course," I might have allowed the origin and evolution of the play to slip away from Memory and be forgotten.

Janet Langhart Cohen's

ANNE & EMMETT

Student Guide

PLAY SUMMARY

Anne & Emmett is an imaginary conversation between Anne Frank and Emmett Till, both victims of racial intolerance and hatred. Frank is the fifteen-year-old Jewish girl whose diary provided a gripping perspective of the Holocaust. Till is the fourteen-year-old African American boy whose brutal murder in Mississippi sparked the modern American Civil Rights Movement.

The one-act play opens with the two teenagers meeting in Memory, an ethereal place where time itself does not exist.

The beyond-the-grave encounter draws startling similarities between the two youths' harrowing experiences and the atrocities against their respective races.

Anne & Emmett reminds us of the roles that race, religion, and ethnicity have played in the past and how hatred and the evil of genocide continue to stalk the world.

Anne Frank and Emmett Till are destined to remain in Memory, locked in an endless conversation until the chain of mankind's bigotry is broken by the grace of illumination and knowledge.

OBJECTIVE

Students will read *Anne & Emmett* and use a wide range of materials drawn from the diversity of human experiences to build an understanding of themselves and diverse cultures; to analyze and interpret significant event patterns and themes in the United States and the world; to acquire new information; and to respond to the needs and demands of society. The play will also serve as a call to action for students to speak out against and oppose bullies who traffic in hatred and abuse toward others because of their race, religion, ethnicity, or orientation.

PROCEDURES

I. Prepare to see the play
   A. Research Jewish history from the days of Slavery in Egypt through the Exodus, the Spanish Inquisition, and the Holocaust, to the present, focusing specifically on the period spanning 1936 to 1945.
      1. Who was Adolf Hitler? How did he come to power? What was his Final Solution?
      2. Did Hitler regard the Jewish people as a race, a religion, or both?
      3. Are Jewish people regarded differently in Germany today? Is Nazism dead in Germany? In America?
      4. What is the difference between race and ethnicity?
   B. Research US history from the days of Slavery through the Civil War, Reconstruction, Jim Crow, and the Civil Rights Movement to Presidents Obama and Trump, focusing specifically on the period spanning 1940 to 1955.
      1. What was the Ku Klux Klan? Does it still exist?
      2. What were the White Citizens' Councils? What is the Council of Conservative Citizens?
      3. What prompted the Civil Rights Movement?
      4. Who were Martin Luther King Jr. and Rosa Parks?
II. Read the play *Anne & Emmett*
III. Answer the discussion questions

IV. Complete the activities and projects
V. See the play *Anne & Emmett*

DISCUSSION QUESTIONS

1. What economic and social factors caused the Germans to turn on the Jewish people?
2. In what ways were the Nazis and Ku Klux Klan the same? How were they different? What were their respective goals, and why did they set them?
3. Did the German people support Hitler's plan to exterminate the Jewish people? If not, why didn't they act to stop him? Why did they remain silent?
4. Why did the American people support the policies and cultural practices of Slavery, Jim Crow, Lynchings, and Segregation? Why did members of Congress fail to stop the South's practice of terrorism against Black people?
5. In the play *Anne & Emmett*, Emmett says, "Fear is just an excuse for hate. If someone says they acted out of fear, they think that makes it more acceptable. They just don't want to admit it, but it's really all about hate." Do you think "fear" is really all about "hate"? Why? Why not?
6. Why did slave owners separate Black families? Why did the Nazi separate Jewish families? What other tactics were used to dominate, dehumanize, and destroy their victims?
7. In the play, Anne says, "Emmett, you're angry, I understand that ... But anger only eats away inside. It doesn't change anything. Just remember, while you were trying to get into the officer clubs, we were trying to stay out of the ovens!" What are your thoughts about this exchange? Give other examples in the play where Anne

and Emmett share their treatment at the hands of their racist oppressors.

8. What roles did faith and religion play in the Holocaust? And in the Civil Rights Movement?
9. In the play, Anne and Emmett have the following exchange:

ANNE: But I could never understand it . . . Everyone loved our music, our art, our dedication to science, medicine, law. We've given so much to the world. I always wondered, what would the world be like without us? Albert Einstein, Marc Chagall, Emma Lazarus, George and Ira Gershwin, Vladimir Horowitz, Justice Louis Brandeis . . . I can count hundreds . . . Jonas Salk, the doctor who discovered the vaccine for polio . . .

EMMETT: Salk? Heard about him all right. Guess he came a little late for me . . .

ANNE: What do you mean "late for you"?

EMMETT: I had polio when I was six years old. It affected my speech somehow . . . made me stutter.

ANNE: I didn't know polio could cause stuttering . . . But you're okay now?

EMMETT: It usually happens when I'm nervous . . . But here in Memory, everything seems to be okay . . .

Anne, what you said about what Jewish people have given the world? I was just thinking . . . what would America—the world, for that matter—be like without our free labor, our music, art, science . . . Frederick Douglass, George Washington Carver, Dr. Charles Drew, W. E. B. Du Bois, Justice Thurgood Marshall, Duke Ellington . . . I mean *the* Duke Ellington! Ida B. Wells, Paul Robeson . . .

It's really sick. America was built on our backs. But once we started to resist . . . demand equal rights, they said, "If you Negroes don't like the way we do things around here, go back to Africa!"

ANNE: The Nazis felt the same way about us, Emmett, but they couldn't send us anywhere. We didn't have a place to go to back to then.

The Holocaust survivors and their families are entitled to receive restitution or reparations from the companies that facilitated and profited from Hitler's genocidal policies. The practice of enslaving Black people and robbing them of their property and livelihood persisted long after the abolition of Slavery, Jim Crow, and Segregation laws. Should there be a policy of reparations for the victims and their surviving families?

10. In the play, Anne and Emmett have the following exchange:

    ANNE: Don't give up hope, Emmett. Remember how we did it.

    EMMETT: Anne, you tell everybody to remember! Everybody tells us to forget!

    "Stop playing the victim. Stop dragging the past around like some dead body in the cemetery. Bury it! It's history!" Black history, I guess. Not American history. We're always told to get over it! Just what's the *it* they want us to get over?

    Why is it important to ask Americans to remember the past? Should Black people forget what's been done to them by white people? Are some things still happening today that were once happening in the past?

11. In your research, did you come across any Jewish or Black inventors? Who were they? What were their contributions?

12. What was the relationship between Jews and Blacks during the Civil Rights Movement? Has that relationship changed? If so, when did it change, and why?
13. Promoting anti-Semitism and denying the existence of the Holocaust is a crime in some European countries. Identify those countries and the penalties imposed.
14. Is hate speech a crime in the United States? What are hate crimes?
15. In the play, Emmett says, "You'd have it made in the shade in America. All you'd have to do is change your name, change your hair and you could pass . . . In America, your religion isn't as important as what color you are. It only matters if you're white. And in America, your people get to be white!" Is Emmett's statement true? Why is Emmett so angry about this? What is the *Bakke* case?
16. Does anti-Semitism exist today? Where? What can be done to stop it?
17. Does racism exist today? Where? What can be done to stop it?
18. Consider the playwright's note in the afterword. Imagine you traveled to Memory. What would you say to Anne and Emmett? What would they say to you?

"A CALL TO ACTION": PRESENT DAY CASES

Research present-day cases of hate and discrimination. What things have changed? What remains the same? How is history something that is living and not relegated to the past?

> Example cases: Trayvon Martin, Matthew Shepard, Laquan McDonald, Eric Garner, George Floyd, Breonna Taylor, Jacob Blake, Merci Mack, Philando Castile

Mass shootings at the Tree of Life Synagogue in Pittsburg, Pennsylvania (October 27, 2018), where 11 congregants were killed and 6 were wounded and, on April 27, 2019, a gunman shot and killed one woman and three others, including the rabbi of the Chabad of Poway Synagogue in Poway, California.

PROJECTS AND ACTIVITIES
1. Prepare a Notebook

    Step 1. Gather the voluminous printed information on the Holocaust, Anne Frank, Emmett Till, and the Civil Rights Movement.

    Step 2. Keep a journal of your feelings and thoughts on things of particular interest or concern to you.

    Step 3. Combine your researched information and journal clips to create a notebook.

    Step 4. Share your notebook with classmates, family, and friends.

2. Vocabulary

    Define the following terms:

    Civil Rights

    Abraham Lincoln
    black gold
    Brown v. Board of Education
    Bull Connor
    bus boycott
    Carolyn Bryant
    Civil Rights Act of 1964
    cotton gin

    Dred Scott decision
    Fannie Lou Hamer
    Frederick Douglass
    Ida B. Wells
    Jackie Robinson
    Jet magazine
    Jim Crow laws
    J. W. Milam

Ku Klux Klan
Loving v. Virginia
Lyndon Baines Johnson
Malcolm X
Mamie Till-Mobley
Martin Luther King Jr.
Mason-Dixon line
Medgar Evers
miscegenation
Rosa Parks

Roy Bryant
reparations
slave states
statute of limitations
sundowner laws
Scottsboro Boys
Underground Railroad
Uncle Mose
Voting Rights Act of 1964

Holocaust

Adolf Hitler
Amsterdam
anti-Semitism
Arbeit macht frei
Aryan
Auschwitz
Babi Yar
Bergen-Belsen
Brown Shirts
Cuba
Dachau
FDR
genocide
gestapo
ghetto
Hakenkreuz
Immigration Act of 1924
Judenrat

Kaddish
Leo Frank
Mein Kampf
Michael Schwerner
MS *St. Louis*
Otto Frank
Nazi
Nuremberg Laws
pogrom
Poland
Promised land
SS
swastika
Talmud
Torah
Third Reich
Ukraine
Westerbork

3. Speeches on Human Rights and Liberation

   Research some of the speeches and essays by prominent authors and describe which ones impressed you the most.

4. Poems Relating to Life in America's South and the Holocaust

   Read and analyze the following poems relating to life in the American South and during the Holocaust. For whom are they written? What purpose do they serve? What emotions are evoked in you when reading them?

Poems

"Mississippi—1955," by Langston Hughes, dedicated to the memory of Emmett Till
"Strange Fruit," sung by Billie Holiday, lyrics by Abel Meeropol
"Memory," by William S. Cohen

> Memory, dimmer now
> as day fades to night,
> and sheets of time lay like
> tattered gauze upon an aging mind.
> I grow old, I grow cold,
> I nod and doze in the warmth
> of glowing coals.
> It seemed just yesterday,
> and I still hear the smashing of glass
> of Kristallnacht, the roar of the Führer
> a shepherd's bark, goose-stepping boots
> on cobblestones, the scream of cars
> on railroad tracks, the crack of gunfire,
> the thump of bodies tossed

wave on wave into open graves
to rot.
Yes, I still remember
seeing flesh turn to ash,
and souls take flight in ovens bright
beyond all Fahrenheit.

And yet, others shout it's
but a devil's trick, a childhood
nightmare at work in an
old man's feeble mind.
A British Bishop, Sudan's Al Bashir,
Iran's Ahmadinejad, they claim I'm mad!
How can I say, "Never Again"
when something never was?
Or "Remember," when there's nothing
to forget?
Has it all come to this—
that new haters can turn a
savage genocide into a rubble
of nothingness?
If humankind is not to die a second time,
then we cannot relent, we must resist!
Memory is all that keeps
the future's Führers from
breaking down our doors.

5. Laws Created to Keep Races Separate

Research some of the laws instituted to deliberately keep races separate. Write or summarize the laws. Document the state in which each law was enacted and the year of origin. Be sure to include the Nuremberg Laws and Jim Crow laws. What circumstances prompted these laws? Are they still on the books today? Have they been modified? Abolished? Keep a journal on which laws inspire you and why.

6. Tackle Stereotypes

   What epithets or derogatory terms are used to describe Jewish and Black people? What do you do when you hear them?

7. Write a Report

   Step 1. Research newspaper and magazine articles on present-day hate crimes and violence.
   Step 2. Keep a journal of your feelings and thoughts on things of particular interest or concern to you as they relate to your research.
   Step 3. Integrate your researched information and journal entries to write a report.
   Step 4. Share your report with classmates, family, and friends.

SUGGESTED READING

Death of Innocence: The Story of the Hate Crime that Changed America by Mamie Till-Mobley

This is the heartbreaking and ultimately inspiring story of one hero, Mamie Till-Mobley, the mother of Emmett Till—an innocent fourteen-year-old African American boy who was in the wrong place at the wrong time and who paid for it with his life. His outraged mother's actions galvanized the Civil Rights Movement, leaving an indelible mark on American racial consciousness.
(*Source:* From the hardcover edition)

Anne Frank: The Diary of a Young Girl
by Anne Frank

Discovered in the attic in which she spent the last years of her life, Anne Frank's remarkable diary has since become a world classic—a powerful reminder of the horrors of war and an eloquent testament to the human spirit. In 1942, with Nazis occupying Holland, a thirteen-year-old Jewish girl and her family fled their home in Amsterdam and went into hiding. For the next two years, until their whereabouts were betrayed to the gestapo, they and another family lived cloistered in the "Secret Annex" of an old office building. Cut off from the outside world, they faced hunger, boredom, the constant cruelties of living in confined quarters, and the ever-present threat of discovery and death. In her diary Anne Frank recorded vivid impressions of her experiences during this period. By turns thoughtful, moving, and amusing, her account offers a fascinating commentary on human courage and frailty and a compelling self-portrait of a sensitive and spirited young woman whose promise was tragically cut short.
(*Source:* From the publisher)

From Rage to Reason: My Life in Two Americas
by Janet Langhart Cohen

From her humble beginning in the projects to her life as a respected journalist and the wildly popular "First Lady" of the Pentagon, Cohen shares her candid and inspiring autobiography, explaining how she used her anger over racism to fuel positive change.
(*Source:* From the publisher)

Race and Reconciliation in America
edited by William S. Cohen and Janet Langhart Cohen

Race and racism have played a divisive and defining role throughout much of America's history. Slavery, Jim Crow laws, Segregation, and Ku Klux Klan terrorism have inflicted deep psychic wounds, social disparities, and economic disadvantages that have diminished the promise of equal rights and opportunities for all.

While much progress in race relations has been made in recent years—including the election of Barack Obama as president of the United States—it's clear that our journey to a postracial era is far from complete. In virtually every measurable category, whether income levels, job opportunities, access to health care, life expectancy, high school diplomas, or incarceration rates, Blacks do not fare well compared to their white counterparts.

The dialogue entitled Race and Reconciliation in America was convened to provide a forum for a long-overdue, open, honest, and constructive discussion among people of good will about the need for the American people to truly grasp the depth of past misdeeds, why the legacies of past oppression persist, and how we can achieve a more fair and just society embodied in the American Dream.
(*Source:* From the publisher)

Night
by Elie Wiesel

The author writes about his experience with his father in the Nazi concentration camps at Auschwitz and Buchenwald from 1944 to 1945, at the height of the Holocaust and toward the end of World

War II. Wiesel was awarded the Nobel Peace Prize in 1986, at which time the Norwegian Nobel committee called him a "messenger to mankind."
(*Source:* Modified from Wikipedia)

Slavery by Another Name: The Re-enslavement of Black Americans from the Civil War to World War II
by Douglas A. Blackmon

The author tells the unfamiliar story of "neoslavery" that reached beyond the de facto slavery of tenant farming and debt peonage. Blackmon first became intrigued by this episode of US history while researching a story for the Wall Street Journal that documented how US Steel Corp. relied on forced Black labor in Alabama coal mines. He discovered that, under laws enacted specifically to intimidate Blacks, tens of thousands of African Americans were arbitrarily arrested, hit with outrageous fines, and charged for the costs of their own arrests. With no means to pay these ostensible "debts," prisoners were sold as forced laborers to coal mines, lumber camps, brickyards, railroads, quarries, and farm plantations. Thousands of other African Americans were simply seized by Southern landowners and compelled into years of involuntary servitude.
(*Source:* From the publisher)

I Am a Star: Child of the Holocaust
by Inge Auerbacher

Inga Auerbacher's childhood was as happy and peaceful as any other German child's—until 1942. By then, the Nazis were in power, and she and her parents were rounded up and sent to a concentration camp. The Auerbachers defied death for three years until they were freed. (*Source:* From the publisher)

The New Jim Crow: Mass Incarceration in the Age of Colorblindness
by Michelle Alexander

This book directly challenges the notion that the election of Barack Obama signaled a new era of colorblindness. With dazzling candor, legal scholar Michelle Alexander argues that "we have not ended racial caste in America; we have merely redesigned it." By targeting Black men through the War on Drugs and decimating communities of color, the US criminal-justice system functions as a contemporary system of racial control—relegating millions to a permanent second-class status—even as it formally adheres to the principle of colorblindness. (*Source:* From the publisher)

Vernon Can Read! A Memoir
by Vernon Jordan

As a young college student in Atlanta, Vernon E. Jordan Jr. had a summer job driving a white banker around town. During the man's postluncheon siestas, Jordan passed the time reading books, a fact that astounded his boss. "Vernon can read!" the man exclaimed to his relatives. Nearly fifty years later, Vernon Jordan—now a senior executive at Lazard Frères, long-time Civil Rights leader, adviser and close friend to presidents and business leaders, and one of the most charismatic figures in America, has written an unforgettable book about his life and times. The story of Vernon Jordan's life encompasses the sweeping

struggles, changes, and dangers of African American life in the civil rights revolution of the second half of the twentieth century.
(*Source:* From the publisher)

The Holocaust Scream: Rachel Rosenberg, Nazi Concentration Camp Survivor; The Holocaust and That Scream
by Rachel Rosenberg, with Robert T. Urban

Are you ready to meet the Polish Anne Frank who survived? Rachel Rosenberg is a Holocaust survivor of four Nazi concentration camps. Learn about her remarkable experience during the Holocaust and its long-term aftereffects.
(*Source:* From the publisher)

SUGGESTED FILMS

The Civil War, series, directed by Ken Burns
Amistad, directed by Steven Spielberg
The Birth of a Nation, directed by D. W. Griffith
Defiance, directed by Edward Zwick
Glory, directed by Edward Zwick
Red Tails, directed by Anthony Hemingway
Roots, TV miniseries, based on the book by Alex Haley
Schindler's List, directed by Steven Spielberg
Sophie's Choice, directed by Alan J. Pakula
The Boy in the Striped Pyjamas, directed by Mark Herman
The Diary of Anne Frank, directed by George Stevens
The Pawnbroker, directed by Sidney Lumet
Slave Narratives: A Folk History of Slavery in the United States, compiled by the Federal Writers' Project as part of the WPA
Unforgivable Blackness, directed by Ken Burns

ACADEMIC STANDARDS
National Curriculum Standards for Social Studies: The Themes of Social Science

Culture—*experiences that provide for the study of culture and cultural diversity*

Civic ideas and practices—*experiences that provide for the study of the ideals, principles, and practices of citizenship in a democratic republic*

Power, authority, and governance—*providing for the study of how people create, interact with, and change structures of power, authority, and governance*

www.ingramcontent.com/pod-product-compliance
Lightning Source LLC
Chambersburg PA
CBHW051133160426
43195CB00014B/2453